MW01122420

Law and Order

by David Conrad

Content and Reading Adviser: Mary Beth Fletcher, Ed.D.
Educational Consultant/Reading Specialist
The Carroll School, Lincoln, Massachusetts

Spyglass
BOOKS

COMPASS POINT BOOKS

Minneapolis, Minnesota

Compass Point Books
3722 West 50th Street, #115
Minneapolis, MN 55410

Visit Compass Point Books on the Internet at *www.compasspointbooks.com*
or e-mail your request to *custserv@compasspointbooks.com*

Photographs ©: skjoldphotographs.com, cover; International Stock/Bob Schatz, 5; Visuals
Unlimited/Mark E. Gibson, 7; Visuals Unlimited/Audrey Gibson, 9; Visuals Unlimited/Bill Kamin, 10;
International Stock/Bill Stanton, 11; Robert Maass/Corbis, 13; Anna Clopet/Corbis, 14;
AFP/Corbis, 15, 19; International Stock/Elliott Smith, 17; Two Coyotes Studio/Mary Foley, 20, 21.

Project Manager: Rebecca Weber McEwen
Editor: Heidi Schoof
Photo Selectors: Rebecca Weber McEwen and Heidi Schoof
Designer: Erin Scott, SARIN creative

Library of Congress Cataloging-in-Publication Data

Conrad, David (David J.), 1967-
  Law and order / by David Conrad.
      p. cm. — (Spyglass books)
Summary: Briefly introduces laws and law enforcement in the
United States.
Includes bibliographical references and index.
  ISBN 0-7565-0383-3 (hardcover)
  1. Police—United States—Juvenile literature. [1. Police. 2. Law
enforcement.] I. Title. II. Series.
  HV8138 .C643 2002
  363.2'3'0973—dc21
                              2002002734

Contents

Rules to Live By

"Treat people the way you want to be treated."

This is a rule that helps people live together happily. People live by many other rules, too.

The rule to raise your hand before talking keeps the class quiet and makes sure everyone is heard.

5

Some rules help people stay *safe*. Some rules help people know how to behave.

Rules can only work if everyone follows them. Police are people who make sure that everyone follows the rules.

A crossing guard helps keep children safe.

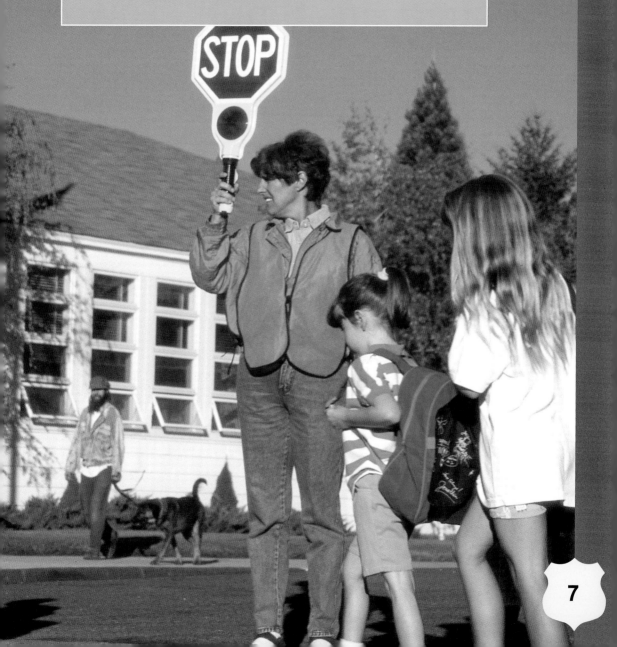

7

Police in Small Towns

In some small towns, there may only be one or two police officers. This is because there are fewer people and less crime than in a big city.

Did You Know?

"Sheriff" is another name for the main police officer in some small towns.

Police in Large Towns

Larger towns and cities may have many police officers. The city may have different *stations* in different places in the city.

Did You Know?

In a city, each police officer has a special job. A detective solves crimes. A traffic officer makes sure people follow the rules of the road. **11**

State Police

Each state has its own police *department*.
State officers can work anywhere in the state.
The Highway Patrol uses state officers to keep people safe on the roads.

State Patrol officers

Did You Know?

When state police officers are in a city or town, they work closely with the town's police officers.

The Nation's Police

Each country has its own police force, too. In the United States, the *FBI*, the *CIA*, and the Secret Service work to protect the country.

FBI training

One of the main jobs of the Secret Service is to protect the president of the United States.

Lawmakers

Every single rule or *law* was once just an idea. Then the people voted on it. If most of the people thought the idea was good, it became a law.

Did You Know?

Sometimes a law gets old or doesn't make sense anymore. Then people vote to get rid of it.

17

Law Breakers

When people do not follow the rules, they go to court. Court is where people who break the law find out what their punishment is.

Lawmakers, the police, and the courts all work together to keep people safe.

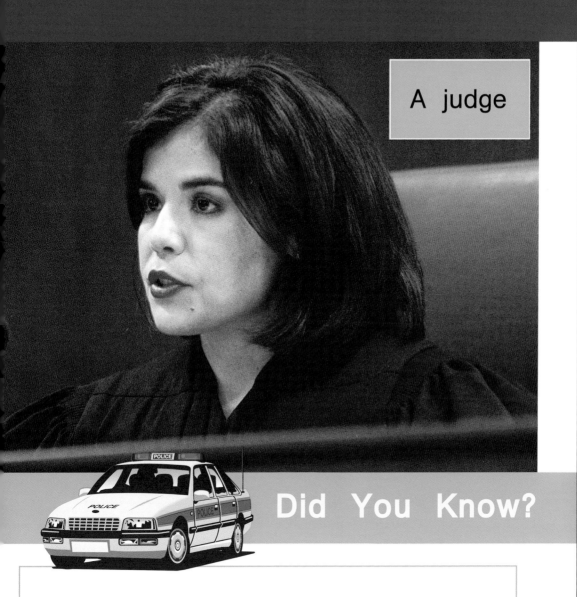

A judge

Did You Know?

In court, the judge is the boss. All of the lawyers and other people in court have to do what the judge says.

Take a Fingerprint

Police use fingerprints as clues. Fingerprints at a crime scene can help police find who did the crime.

You will need:
- a glass
- scotch tape
- a towel

1. Wipe the glass clean.

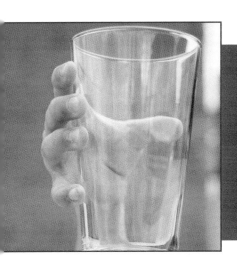

2. Hold the glass in your hand.

3. Press a piece of tape over the fingerprint and carefully lift it off.

4. Can you see the fingerprint?

Glossary

CIA–the Central Intelligence Agency. This part of the government learns about other countries.

department–a group of police and the people who work with them

FBI–the Federal Bureau of Investigation. This part of the government does police work for the United States.

law–a rule that tells people what to do or not to do

safe–out of danger

station–a building where the police and their helpers work

Learn More

Books

Jeunesse, Gallimard, and Daniel Moignot. *Fire Fighting*. Illustrated by Daniel Moignot. New York: Scholastic, 1997.

Lima Beans Would Be Illegal: Children's Ideas of a Perfect World. Compiled and illustrated by Robert Bender. New York: Dial Books for Young Readers, 2000.

Ryon Quiri, Patricia. *The Bill of Rights*. New York: Children's Press, 1998.

Web Sites

pbskids.org/dragonflytv/knowhow/knowhow_stopthief_textonly2.htm

www.pbs.org/democracy/kids/mygovt/police.html

Index

GR: H

Word Count: 229

From David Conrad

I am a scientist who lives in Colorado. I like to climb mountains, square dance, and play with my pet frog, Clyde.